KINGSTEIGNTON
COLLECTION

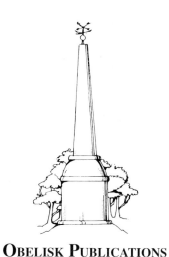

OBELISK PUBLICATIONS

Other Books in this Series

Some Other Obelisk Publications

First Published in 1994 by Obelisk Publications
2 Church Hill, Pinhoe, Exeter, Devon
Designed by Chips and Sally Barber
Typeset by Sally Barber
Printed in Great Britain by
Ashley House, Marsh Barton, Exeter

For further details of these or any of our extensive
Devon titles, please contact us at 2 Church Hill,
Pinhoe, Exeter, EX4 9ER, Tel: (0392) 468556.

ISBN: 0 946651 87 6

Over the years I have collected many old pictures and postcards of Kingsteignton. This book has been put together so you may peruse and enjoy the village as it was of yesteryear. We start by looking towards Kingsteignton from Breakneck Hill in the mid 1930s when the brickworks of Hexter and Humpherson formed a prominent feature in the landscape. During their construction, in 1889, the local press reported that "the residents of Kingsteignton are viewing with pride the building of the brick and pottery works near their pretty village". The village has changed somewhat since the correspondent penned that account and the brickworks were pulled down in the early 1970s. However, the cream-coloured bricks produced there can still be seen in countless buildings throughout the South West.

A view of Newton Road captured by the camera around 1925. The Devon General Omnibus and Touring Co. Ltd. opened their garage to the left in 1921 where it served as a repair workshop for some 38 years. Mr N. V. Stowe traded as a chemist from the present electrical shop of C. P. Stone, and across the road building land was being offered for sale.

On 12 November 1887 Lord Clifford unveiled the Jubilee Memorial Fountain at Oakford. Erected at a cost of £60, it was designed by a Mr Wyatt of Torquay and consisted of horse, cattle and dog troughs with a lamp post as its centre-piece.

By the late 1920s Mr J. Honywill had built a new butcher's shop at Oakford and the Midland Bank had established a branch next door, which opened on Mondays, Wednesdays and Fridays.

Another view of the Fountain taken from the opposite direction in 1947. The Co-operative Society's Fountain branch was still prospering and advertising hoardings fronted the yard of the Eddison Steam Roller Company.

The present Church House was built in 1864 as a Master's residence for the National School. The school itself still retains the Anglican links but under the name of St Michael's C of E Primary School.

Mr T. C. Ward paused from his deliveries to be photographed near Victoria Terrace in about 1910. The family's shop in Fore Street still trades under the name of W. A. Ward & Son although now under the proprietorship of Mr M. Bearne.

Fore Street, Kingsteignton

There was no danger from traffic when taking a group photograph in Fore Street in 1905. Mr W. H. Uff was agent for Ridgway's tea whilst on the opposite side of the road number 10 possessed a fine capping of thatch.

FORE ST KINGSTEIGNTON 17258

Some twenty or so years later and John Trethewey was delivering firewood from his donkey cart. Mr Edwin Good had opened a shop at number 8 and had his hardware goods displayed on the pavement whilst Fry's cocoa was on sale at the Star Bakery.

BELL INN, KINGSTEIGNTON.

WILLIAMS'S
BELL INN
FREE HOUSE

(Opposite) The Bell Inn has long been a favourite watering hole for many villagers and is shown here in the late 1920s not long after Mr Williams had taken over as mine host. To the left of the picture one can see that the course of the brook was uncovered right up to its junction with Fore Street.

The close grouped cottages, which used to flank the Fairwater leat alongside Berry Lane, provided a favourite view for photographers in the early years of this century. The cottages on the right were demolished in 1935 under a slum clearance programme, which saw many of the older cob dwellings in the village disappear.

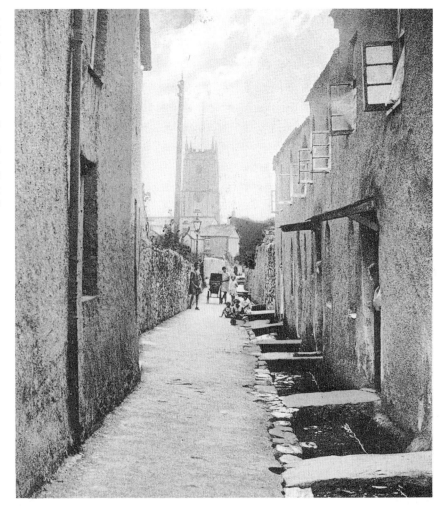

KINGSTEIGNTON

Standing on a prominent corner site, Berry Farm is one of many farmhouses, which used to be found in the village centre. When this picture was taken, Mr Tom Edwards ran his dairy from the farm, his cattle being kept in fields at Oakymead. In those days the streets of the village resounded with the noise of cattle being driven back from the fields for milking in the early hours of the morning.

(Opposite) A view of Fore Street looking west in the early 1900s when gas lamps lit the village streets. Thatched cottages fronted the road between numbers 43 and 49 and the Dewdrop Inn was only joined to Berry Farm at ground floor level. The Dewdrop Inn, like the other cottages shown here, was once the property of Lord Clifford. It was sold to the tenant, Mr A. Holman, for £1,375 in 1923.

A Burrell Cornishman traction engine, with threshing machine in tow, had just crashed through the hedge at the bottom of Ware Hill when pictured here in 1912. The news of the accident rapidly attracted an inquisitive crowd from the village.

(Opposite) Now divided into two dwellings, known as The Chantry and Elmfield, this house was originally built as a vicarage for the Rev. Thomas Whipham by John Rendle of Teignmouth. Started in 1815 it was "nearing completion" in 1821 according to a reply given to the Bishop of Exeter. In its original form it has been described as "one of the very best examples of cottage orne genre of the country".

A much changed view of the Teign estuary from Teignmouth Road in the late 1920s. The electricity power station in Newton Abbot was opened by the Torquay Corporation in 1924. The demand for this new source of power was such that in later years extensions added twin chimneys and a cooling tower, which formed impressive local landmarks until their demolition in 1974. At the time of this photo there was no viaduct spanning the saltmarshes and smaller fields with tree-lined hedges bordered the river.

(Opposite) For many years the Passage House Inn has provided a stop-off for riverborne travellers. Many of these used to be the lightermen who crewed the barges taking clay down the river to Teignmouth. It was an extremely hard occupation and the lightermen acquired a reputation for toughness and unquenchable thirsts. They were known to give precedence to filling their cider jars over meeting a high tide at Teignmouth.

HACKNEY KINGSTEIGNTON 26001

19

The Lychgate to the churchyard remains little changed but the trees, which lined the church path, have long been felled. One can just see the thatched roof of one of the old almshouses which used to stand in the churchyard on the right of the picture.

(Opposite) There has probably been a church on this site since shortly after the foundation of the village in the early eighth century. The first written record occurs in the register of St Osmund of Salisbury. Dated about 1108, it confirms the appropriation of the "Church of Teignton together with the chapels and tithes pertaining to it" to Salisbury Cathedral.

Kingsteignton Church

The Rev Percival Jackson is seen here preparing to unveil the new war memorial to honour those who had fallen in the Great War. People are often puzzled why the Kingsteignton memorial bears the dates 1914–1919 when the armistice was signed in 1918. The explanation for this is that many communities lost servicemen in the period between November 1918 and the peace treaty in June 1919 through the effects of injury and in the ill-fated Archangel expedition to aid the White Russians. Where this was the case, the later date of 1919 was used.

A more cheerful celebration of the end of the Great War where a procession can be seen parading along Greenhill Road. Note the thatched cottages which stood between number 6 and Berry Farm.

Haytor View remains little changed today but most of the buildings along the same side of the road have disappeared. Farther down the road on the opposite side is Brookside, once the residence of Mr J. Whidbourne JP. He was Master of the South Devon Hunt and used Brookside as a hunting cottage, stabling his horses across the road where a bungalow now stands. A banker and solicitor, he provided funds to secure a playground for the children of the National School.

By 1950 the wall to the left of the picture was all that remained of Margery Farm but Tom Whitear was still delivering milk around the village with his handcart.

Crossley Moor, Kingsteignton CDS24512

Chapman and Son, Dawlish

26

The rapid march of development had yet to reach Crossley Moor and Mr Bennett's cottage still stood at the crossroads when viewed here in 1927. Moorgates, where Rydon Estate now stands, was one of many allotment fields in the village, which would be filled with men planting potatoes in springtime.

(Opposite) One could gaze across the allotment field towards the moors when sat beside the brook in the mid-1950s. The upper windows of Higher Mill House were in fact bricked up when this picture was taken but the brushwork of an imaginative decorator gave the impression that the panes of glass were still there.

OAKFORD. KINGSTEIGNTON.

28

GESTRIDGE R^D KINGSTEIGNTON.

The junction of Broadway Road and Gestridge Road showing the York lamppost, which commemorated a visit by the Duke of York in 1899. Following the formation of the village Liberal Association in 1908, premises were acquired at the end of Knowles View Terrace to serve as its headquarters. Not to be left behind, the Conservative Association opened the former Drill Hall in Broadway Road as a Unionist Club in 1909, and the building now serves as the Kingsteignton Youth Centre.

(Opposite) When Lord Clifford sold off most of his Kingsteignton estate in 1923, John Osborne purchased a site beside Knowles View Terrace, for the princely sum of £90, where he set up a petrol station selling Pratt's spirit. The business was purchased by the Burridge family in 1951 and now takes in part of the adjoining terrace.

29

One of the greatest changes witnessed after the end of the First World War was the growth in motorised public transport. Charabancs owned by companies such as Devon General provided a means of access to places that could not be reached by bus or train. This picture shows members of the Congregational Church (now United Reformed) about to depart for Bude from the Devon General Garage in Newton Road in 1925. To the right of the picture one can just make out the old steam laundry which used to stand next to the present Plymco Homemaker site.

Another charabanc outing, this time showing members of the Liberal Club setting off in 1921 in a vehicle hired from the South Devon Garage and Motor Touring Company.

Gestridge Road as viewed in 1950 with Mr W. Bartlett standing in his shop doorway. For many years the Bartlett family sold paint and decorating materials from this shop, which was originally built as the Kingsteignton branch of the local Co-operative Society. Today, like many other former shops in the village, it has been converted to residential use.

GESTRIDE, KINGSTEIGNTON.

The Wesleyan Chapel in Gestridge Road was still thriving when pictured here in the late 1920s. Older villagers will remember George Beer's bakery, which was located next door. His yellow brick bakehouse at the rear is now used by Newton Abbot Plumbing Supplies. You might note the spelling error on this postcard!

33

KINGS TEIGNTON. K.11.   EXETER ROAD.

Village builder Mr D. H. Howe had just completed his development of the northern side of Ley Lane when this picture was taken in the mid 1930s. Such was the scarcity of traffic there was no need for a pavement.

(Opposite) Not a car in sight in this view of Exeter Road taken around 1914. This stretch of road from Chudleigh Corner to Imperial Building was cut through by the local Turnpike Trust in the 1830s. The plan incorporated a new road across the marshes from south of the village to Newton Abbot and paved the way for the rapid growth of the village in later years.

ABBROOK TEA GARDENS

BED and BREAKFAST
"LIGHT REFRESHMENTS"

GARAGE

COLD LUNCHEONS
CREAM TEAS
PLAIN TEAS
SALADS

BED &
BREAKFAST

CAR PARK
DRIVE IN

(Top, opposite) By the late 1920s the village was developing the long drawn out plan we see today. Mr A. Lewis had opened a grocery shop at 156 Exeter Road to cater for people living at the northern end of the village and later added the services of a Post Office.

(Bottom, opposite) An oak tree stood at the end of Strap Lane and passing motorists could stop for a cream tea at Abbrook Tea Gardens when viewed here in 1939. Five Lanes had only four lanes until the Turnpike Trust cut a new road through Millpark in the mid 1830s and plans for the scheme show that the name Strap Lane was applied to the whole stretch of road from Abbrook to Echogate.

((Above) Soldiers of the Royal 1st Devon Imperial Yeomanry practising their arms drill during their annual camp in May 1908. Compulsory church attendance swelled the congregation at St Michael's by over 400 during the period of the camp. This shot was taken looking towards Great Hill from what is now the sports field of Teign School at Lambparks.

(Right) By the early 1920s the greater part of the congregation of the Brethren chapel at Sandygate lived in the main village. A decision was made to dispose of the chapel, shown here, and use the proceeds of the sale to build new premises in Exeter Road. However, the Sandygate members preferred to worship closer to home and secured a site on the eastern side of Sandygate Lane where a small wooden hall was built. In later years they moved again into a larger hall located a few yards up the road on the western side but dwindling membership eventually led to the closure of the third chapel to be built in Sandygate.

Fosterville Lodge dates from the 1820s when it was built as a lodge to Ugbrooke Park. Originally a two roomed dwelling, more recent additions have increased the size of the accommodation it offered Mrs Tolley and her family when this picture was taken.

Horses still provided the power to pull carts and machinery at Fosterville Farm when Mr and Mrs J. White posed for this photograph with some of their workers in the early 1920s. Old maps of the parish show the farm spelling as Fostiville, reflecting a pronunciation still used by many older natives of the village.

The crew of the Kingsteignton Auxiliary Fire Service were ready for any emergency when pictured here at Gallows Cross in 1942. Perhaps their most exciting call out during the war occurred in January 1941 when a German bomber dropped over 100 incendiary bombs near the village. Fortunately the bombs fell on snow-covered fields between Longford Lane and Coombesend and no houses were damaged. The firemen were: W. Lang, W. Pitts, H. Murrin, J. Quantick, W. Bovey, A. Scott, H. Haynes, R. Perryman, D. Hughes, F. Herd and H. Watts.

(Opposite) Teignbridge House, pictured on the left was one of the few gentry residences to be found in the parish. In its heyday it possessed a riverside boathouse and landing stage. It was demolished in the mid 1960s when E.C.C. extended their nearby clay quarry.

TEIGNBRIDGE KINGSTEIGNTON 24511

The unique custom of roasting a ram annually at Whitsuntide gave rise to the inhabitants of Kingsteignton being given the nickname of Ramroasters. By the late nineteenth century the Fair had degenerated into a somewhat rowdy occasion, characterised by drinking and fighting. Reforms made by a Committee headed by the Rev P. Jackson were introduced to "subdue the coarser qualities of the black sheep of the parish".

One of the reforms introduced by the Committee was that of a cart horse show where the working horses of the village were paraded in all their fine harness and brasses. A young George Tolley is seen here outside Lower Mill, with one of Miller Daw's horses, having just completed his preparations for the Fair.

Prior to its roasting on the day of the Fair, the carcass of the unfortunate ram was paraded through the village streets on a decorated cart at the head of a procession.

Kingsteignton RFC lifted the Devon Junior Cup in 1931 when they defeated North Tawton. It was sweet revenge for the "Cherry and Whites" who had lost in the previous year's final to the same team. The winning line up included: J. Mudge, F. Harris, A. Selley, F. Discombe, C. Scott, E. Rice. Back row: S. Napper, J. Barber, Hepper. Middle row: E.Scott, G. Steer, P. Cornall, W. Holwill, H. Mudge, J. Knapman, S. Frost. Seated: P. Bovey, C. Spear

Jim Knapman went on to play the professional code for Rochdale Hornets, following in the footsteps of another former Kingsteignton player 'Dickie' Paddon. Paddon scored two goals in the Hornets' victory over Hull in the 1922 Rugby League Challenge Cup Final.

In July 1930 a meeting was convened at the Church School where a new association football club called Kingsteignton Athletic was formed. It was to be non-political, unsectarian and run for the welfare of the village.
This line up shows the reserve team in 1932/33 at their original home at Garage Lawn (where St Michael's Road now stands) and reads: Back Row: M. Wallis, T. Nicholls, S. Wallis, G. Henley, F. Hamlyn, P. Winser, F. Ellis. Middle Row: J. Moore, W. Bovey, R. Steer, D. Widdicombe, A. Sanders, H. Mason. Seated: J. Steer, P. Lee

Summer sport in the village was represented by a successful cricket team in 1935, which won the Newton District cup. The team included many fine allrounders in its line up such as Phil Joslin, who made a name for himself as goal keeper with Torquay United and Cardiff City. This photograph was taken at their Oakford Lawn pitch and shows: Back Row: S. Carnell, A. Field, W. Sanders, H. Coombe, F. Hamlyn, J. Edworthy, R. Scott. Middle Row: W. Diamond, L. Hill, A. Johnson, C. Kerslake, H. Mudge, J. Cook, P. Joslin, W. Davis. Seated: M. Johnson, R. Mitchell.

When the local clay companies refused to meet the demands for better conditions and trade union recognition, a bitter strike broke out in June 1913 throwing the industry into turmoil. Such was the intensity of feeling some workers resorted to sabotaging equipment at the pits. Bolstered by public support and fund raising marches the workers held out for 11 weeks until their demands were finally met. A group of miners is shown here with Mr J. Jones of the Gas Workers and General Workers Union, who assisted them in their struggle.

I hope that you have enjoyed this nostalgic trip down 'Memory Lane' to look at a Kingsteignton of a bygone age. The photographers who took these pictures probably never imagined that things would change so much through the passing years. No doubt there will be more changes yet to come!